W9-ACC-667

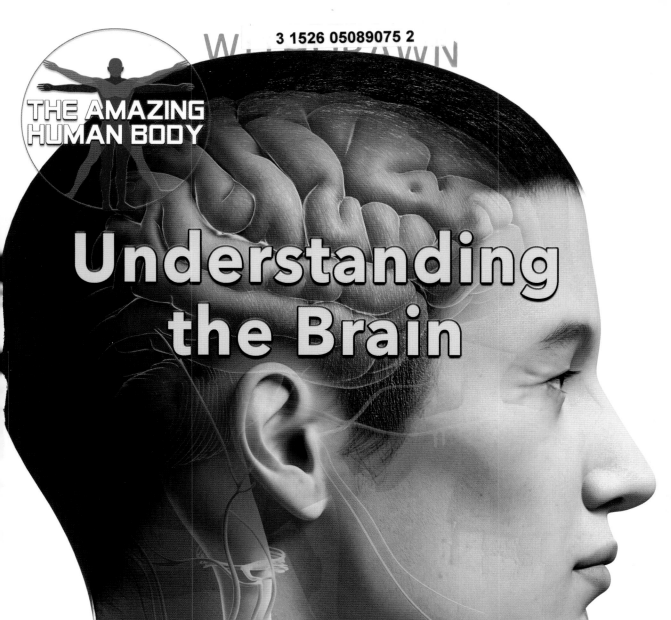

THE AMAZING HUMAN BODY

Understanding the Brain

Edited by
Joanne Randolph

Enslow Publishing

101 W. 23rd Street
Suite 240
New York, NY 10011
USA

enslow.com

This edition published in 2018 by:
Enslow Publishing, LLC.
101 W. 23rd Street, Suite 240
New York, NY 10011

Library of Congress Cataloging-in-Publication Data

Names: Randolph, Joanne, editor.
Title: Understanding the brain / edited by Joanne Randolph.
Description: New York, NY : Enslow Publishing, 2018. | Series: The amazing human body | Audience: Grade level 5-8. | Includes bibliographical references and index.
Identifiers: LCCN 2017001860 | ISBN 9780766090033 (library bound book) | ISBN 9780766090019 (pbk. book) | ISBN 9780766090026 (6 pack)
Subjects: LCSH: Brain—Juvenile literature. | Neurosciences—Juvenile literature.
Classification: LCC QP376 .U53 2018 | DDC 612.8/2—dc23
LC record available at https://lccn.loc.gov/2017001860

Printed in China

To Our Readers: We have done our best to make sure all website addresses in this book were active and appropriate when we went to press. However, the author and the publisher have no control over and assume no liability for the material available on those websites or on any websites they may link to. Any comments or suggestions can be sent by email to customerservice@enslow.com.

Photos Credits: Cover, p. 1 Sebastian Kaulitzki/Shutterstock.com; ksenia_bravo/Shutterstock.com (series logo); p. 3, back cover Tusiy/Shutterstock.com; pp. 4, 12, 22, 30 Romanova Natali/Shutterstock.com (neurons), SUWIT NGAOKAEW/Shutterstock.com (chemical structure background); p. 5 Universal History Archive/Universal Images Group/Getty Images; p. 6 Nan Skyblack/Shutterstock.com; p. 7 Photo Researchers/Science Source/Getty Images; p. 9 Zephyr/Science Photo Library/Getty Images; p. 10 Ted Thai/The LIFE Picture Collection/Getty Images; p. 13 Alan Gesek/Stocktrek Images/Getty Images; p. 14 wetcake/DigitalVision Vectors/Getty Images; pp. 17, 24 Will & Deni Mcintyre/Science Source/Getty Images; p. 18 Christian Science Monitor/Getty Images; p. 20 Monkey Business Images/Shutterstock.com; p. 23 Thierry Berrod, Mona Lisa Production/Science Source; p. 26 Photobac//Shutterstock.com; p. 28 Merbe/E+/Getty Images; p. 29 George Doyle/Thinkstock; p. 31 Universal Images Group/Getty Images; P. 32 James Holmes/Science Photo Library/Getty Images; p. 33 Bruce Rolff/Shutterstock.com; p. 35 Mindy w.m. Chung/Shutterstock.com; p. 37 Hank Morgan/Science Source/Getty Images; p. 38 royaltystockphoto.com/Shutterstock.com; p. 40 Andrey_Popov/Shutterstock.com; pp. 42-43 Yusuf D/Shutterstock.com; pp. 44-45 Science Source.

Article Credits: Dr. Eric H. Chudler, "A Computer in Your Head?" *Odyssey*; Jeanne Miller, "Mary, Mary, Quite Contrary, How Do Your Dendrites Grow?" *Odyssey*; Kathiann M. Kowalski, "'Rewiring' the Brain," *Odyssey*; Trudee Romanek, "The Mysteries of Sleep," *Ask*.

CONTENTS

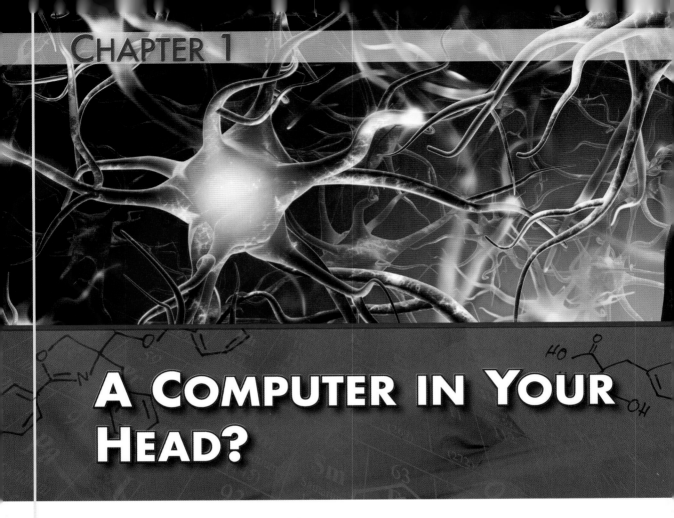

CHAPTER 1

A COMPUTER IN YOUR HEAD?

What has billions of individual pieces, trillions of connections, weighs about 3 pounds (1.4 kilograms), and works on electrochemical energy? If you guessed a mini-computer, you're wrong. If you guessed the human brain, you're correct! The human brain: a mass of white-pink tissue that allows you to ride a bike, read a book, laugh at a joke, and remember your friend's phone number. And that's just for starters. Your brain controls your emotions, appetite, sleep, heart rate, and breathing. Your brain is who you are and everything you will be.

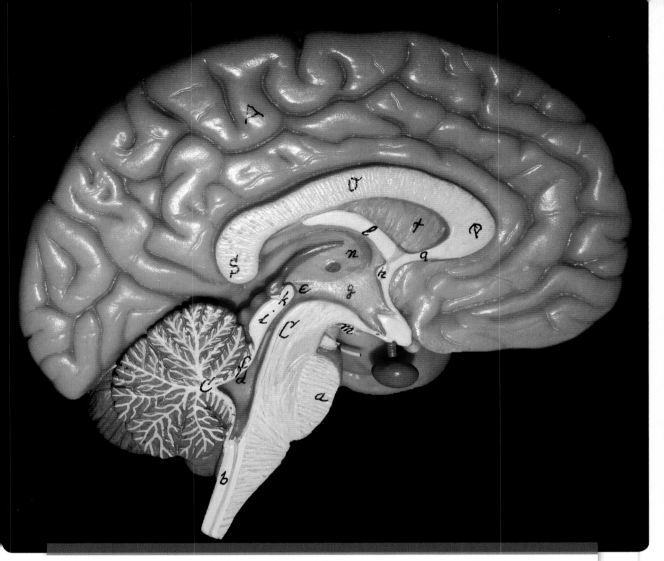

This is a cross-section of a human brain. The larger outer part is called the cortex. The small round part with branch-like structures is the cerebellum. All the parts of the brain have different jobs to do.

The amazing brain has been compared to many different objects and devices—from a spiderweb to a clock to a telephone switchboard. Nowadays, people like to compare it to a computer. Is your brain really like the metal box that hums on your desk? Let's look at the similarities and differences between the two.

Computers help us do all sorts of tasks, such as looking up information, but it took a human brain to design computers to begin with. The human brain is an amazing and complex system.

GOING TO THE SOURCE

Computers and brains both need energy. Plug your computer into the wall, push a button, and it will get the power it needs to run. Pull the plug and it will shut down. Your brain operates in a different way. It gets its energy in the form of glucose from the food you eat. Your diet also provides essential materials, such as vitamins and minerals, for proper brain function. Unlike a computer, your brain has no off switch. Even when you are asleep, your brain is active.

Although computers and brains are powered by different types of energy, they both use electrical signals to transmit information. Computers send electrical signals through wires to control devices.

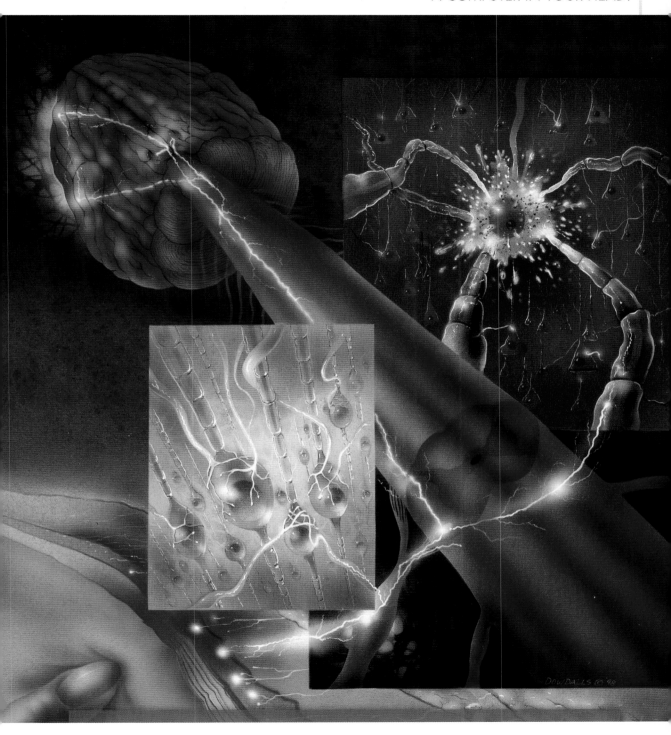

This illustration gives you a sense of how the nerves send
signals to tell the brain that the skin has been touched.

Your brain also sends electrical signals, but it sends them through nerve cells, called neurons. Signals in neurons transfer information to other neurons and control glands, organs, or muscles.

There are fundamental differences in the way information is transferred through electrical circuits in a computer and through nerve cells in your brain. When a computer is turned on, electrical signals either reach parts of the machine or they do not. In other words, the computer uses switches that are either on or off.

In the nervous system, neurons are more than just on or off. An individual neuron may receive information from thousands of other neurons. The region where information is transferred from one neuron to another is called the synapse. A small gap between neurons is located at the synapse. When information is transferred from one neuron to another, molecules of chemicals, called neurotransmitters, are released from the end of one neuron. The neurotransmitters travel across the gap to reach a receiving neuron, where they attach to special structures called receptors. This results in a small electrical response within the receiving neuron. However, this small response does not mean that the message will continue. Remember, the receiving neuron may be getting thousands of small signals at many synapses. Only when the total signal from all of these synapses exceeds a certain level will a large signal, or an action potential, be generated and the message continue.

FORM AND FUNCTION

Despite the differences in the way messages are sent through wires and neurons, computers and brains perform many similar functions. For example, both can store memories—computers do it on chips, disks, and CD-ROMs, and brains use neuronal circuits throughout the brain. Both computers and brains can be modified to perform new tasks. New hardware and software can be installed in computers to add additional memory and programs. The brain undergoes continual modification and can learn new things. The brain can sometimes rewire itself when necessary! For example, after some kinds of brain injuries, undamaged brain tissue can take over functions previously performed by the injured area. I'd like to see a computer rewire itself after its hard drive failed!

Computers and brains both have the ability to monitor their surroundings and respond with behavior to manipulate their environment. Sensors attached to computers can sample temperature, humidity, and light levels. Computers can be programmed to control heaters, lights, and other equipment in response to the information they receive. Your brain is also connected to sensors or

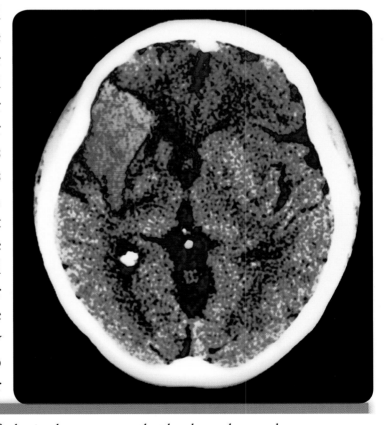

This CT scan of a brain shows an area that has been damaged, in orange, because of a stroke. When certain areas of the brain are damaged, other healthy areas can assume their roles.

The skull protects the fragile brain from injuries. Humans are born with forty-four plates in the skull. Over time, these pieces fuse together to form larger plates. An adult human has twenty-two bones in the skull, including the bones in the face.

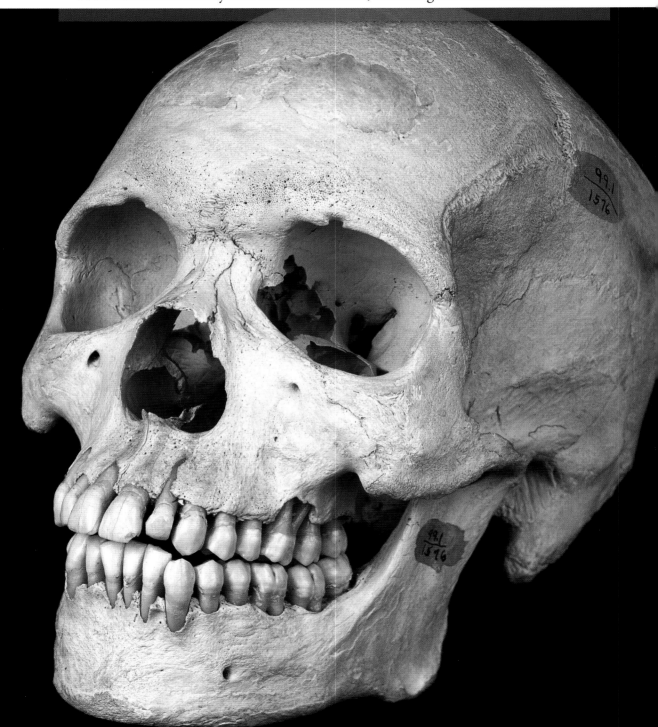

receptors in your eyes, ears, nose, mouth, and skin. Your nervous system may respond to sensory information automatically, or it may cause you to alter your behavior. For example, if a room is too cold, your brain might send signals to muscles to get you to move to a warmer place or to put on a sweater.

The delicate contents inside your computer are protected by a hard cover. Your skull provides a similar function for your brain. The external and internal components of computers and brains are all susceptible to damage. If you drop your computer, infect it with a virus, or leave it on during a huge power surge, your precious machine will likely be on its way to the repair shop. When damaged parts are replaced or the virus-caused damage is removed, your computer should be as good as new. Unfortunately, brains are not as easy to repair. They are fragile and there are no replacement parts to fix damaged brain tissue. However, hope is on the horizon for people with brain damage and neurological disorders, as scientists investigate ways to transplant nerve cells and repair injured brains.

THE BIG DIFFERENCE

No doubt the biggest difference between a computer and your brain is consciousness. Although it may be difficult for you to describe consciousness, you know you are here. Computers do not have such awareness. Although computers can perform extraordinary computational feats at astounding speeds, they do not experience the emotions, dreams, and thoughts that are an essential part of what makes us human. At least not yet! Current research in artificial intelligence is moving toward developing emotional capabilities in computers and robots.

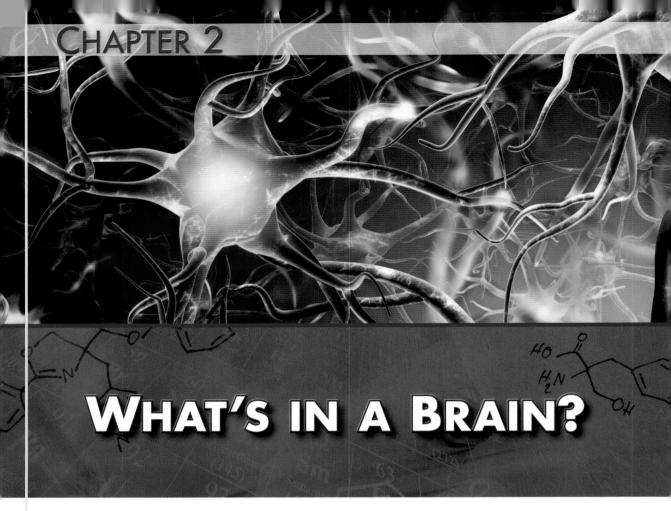

CHAPTER 2

WHAT'S IN A BRAIN?

We now know a little bit about how the brain works, but what exactly is the brain? The brain is part of our central nervous system. It works with the spine and our nerves, called the peripheral nervous system, to control every part of our lives. It controls bodily functions such as making your heart beat, or telling you to scratch your nose, to helping you form opinions (Do you like that sweater your mom just bought for you?) and to make decisions.

THE BRAIN

The brain is made up of three main parts. These are the forebrain, the midbrain, and the hindbrain. The forebrain is made up of the cerebrum, the thalamus, and the hypothalamus. The midbrain is made up of the tectum and tegmentum. The hindbrain is made up of the cerebellum, pons, and medulla.

The cerebrum is the biggest part of the brain. It is divided into lobes: the frontal lobe, the parietal lobe, the occipital lobe, and the temporal lobe. The frontal lobe has to do with reasoning, planning, parts of speech, movement, emotions, and problem solving. The parietal lobe is in charge of movement, orientation, recognition, and interacting with the surroundings. The occipital lobe is mainly engaged with vision and things vision-related, while the temporal lobe is focused on hearing, speech, and memory.

Brain Surface Anatomy

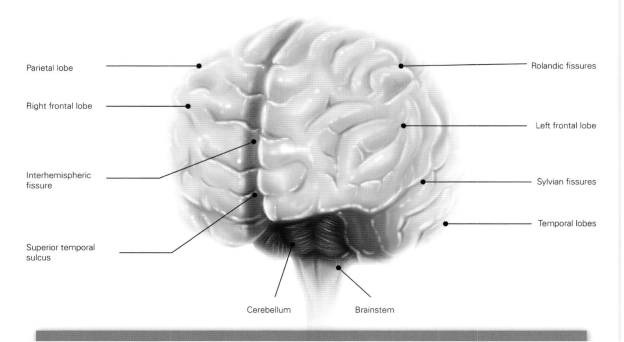

Parietal lobe

Right frontal lobe

Interhemispheric fissure

Superior temporal sulcus

Rolandic fissures

Left frontal lobe

Sylvian fissures

Temporal lobes

Cerebellum   Brainstem

This diagram of the surface of the brain shows the different lobes as well as the fissures, or grooves, that divide the lobes.

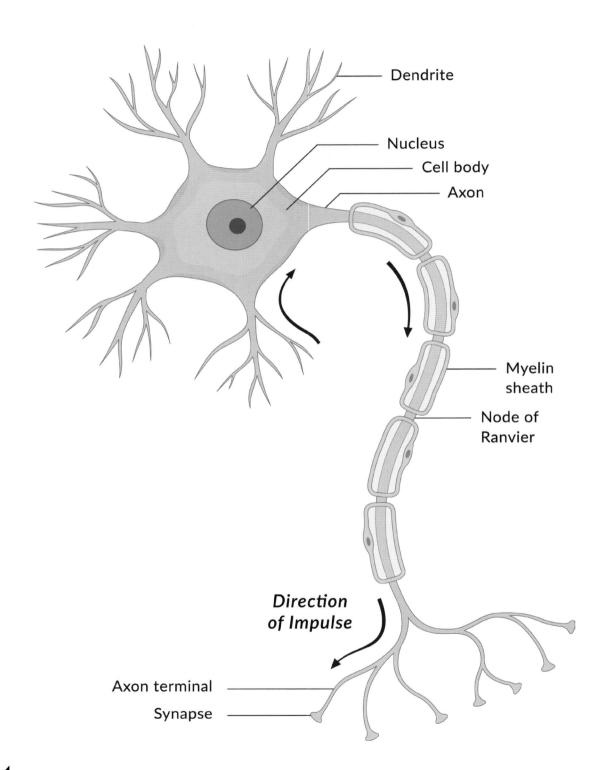

Dendrite

Nucleus

Cell body

Axon

Myelin sheath

Node of Ranvier

Direction of Impulse

Axon terminal

Synapse

All of these tissues are made up of cells and many of them are nerve cells. These cells are sending messages from the brain, our central processing unit, out to the rest of the body and bringing new information back to the brain.

DENDRITES: MAKING THE CONNECTION

So, now let's focus on the neurons that are the messengers for the brain. Professor Marian Diamond, a neuroanatomist at the University of California at Berkeley, pictures the nerve cell, or neuron, as a miniature tree, with the trunk splitting into branches that divide again and again until the process finishes in small leafy twigs. Along a neuron's "twigs" are synapses, across which a message from another neuron can pass. The more branches, the more synapses; the more synapses, the more information the brain can receive!

Dendrites are to nerve cells what fingers are to hands. Extending from the palm, fingers receive sensory information from the objects with which they come in contact. In the case of dendrites, those objects are other nerve cells, but, unlike with fingers, touching isn't necessary. Messages pass from the axon of one nerve cell to the dendrite of another, across a narrow gap called a "synaptic cleft."

A neuron has an axon that carries messages away from the cell body and dendrites that receive messages from other neurons. The place where the transmitting axon of one neuron meets the receiving dendrite of another neuron is called a synapse.

RATS AS MODELS

How does a neuron get more branches? Before the 1960s, science taught us that, except as a result of injury, the brain could not change its structure. "At about that time," says Diamond, "Donald Hebb, at McGill University, was observing his children's rats. He thought that they should be able to run mazes better than laboratory rats who just sat in cages. It made sense, but nobody had ever quantified it. He tested them and, sure enough, the rats that were allowed to run around in a big house with lots of friends and lots of toys solved mazes better than those poor little rats in solitary confinement."

A group of researchers in Berkeley was determined to see what was going on in the brains of those rats. "They designed experimental conditions, with an 'enriched' environment— twelve rats in a large cage with toys—and an 'impoverished' environment— one rat in a small cage with no toys. The control group was housed three to a cage, the way they're normally housed in a lab."

Later, Diamond examined the brain tissue of these rats under a microscope. "We found that the cortex had increased its dimensions with enrichment and decreased them with impoverishment," she says. Further examination showed that dendrites in some parts of the cerebral cortex had developed more branches, and thus those parts of the brain had grown.

Professor William Greenough, a neurobiologist at the University of Illinois at Urbana-Champaign, carried out similar experiments and found that the rats in the stimulating environment had about 20 to 25 percent more dendrites on the average nerve cell than those rats housed separately. Does that mean those rats were smarter? They learned mazes more easily than the solitary rats, one sign of intelligence. Greenough says, "If you grow up with lots of information processed, lots of opportunities for learning, you have a brain that is more complex, that has more wiring, more connections between nerve cells."

Rats are often used in medical research because their genetics and behavior are very similar to humans. Scientists can study how people learn, how drugs will impact diseases, and other things.

Both groups did follow-up work showing that the brain's ability to change its structure in response to experience continues throughout life. Later studies by others showed that these findings translated well to human brains.

MENTAL AND PHYSICAL ENRICHMENT

So the question is: What kinds of experiences must we offer our brain to increase its ability to learn? "Both mental and physical activity seem to be important—both affect the brain," says Greenough. The Urbana-Champaign group designed an experiment to study this idea. In one cage, they created an obstacle course that offered

People need to be exposed to new things in order to build brain matter. One way to do this is to visit science fairs and exhibits showcasing new technology.

learning with little exercise. In other cages, they provided wheels and treadmills that offered exercise with little learning. The control group merely sat in cages, with no opportunities for learning or exercise.

As expected, the animals that learned new skills increased the number of synapses. Additionally, the animals that merely exercised and didn't learn anything didn't increase the number of synapses. However, they did add capillaries to their brains. Additional capillaries means increased blood flow.

"So you can see," Greenough continues, "that there are important and complementary effects of learning and of exercise upon the brain, with learning affecting, more or less, the connections between the cells and the brain's wiring diagram, and exercise affecting, among other things, the blood supply to the brain. You need both."

Active participation rather than passive observation is important for dendrite growth.

"If you have rats watching other rats in enrichment, the watchers' brains aren't changing," Diamond says. Interacting with the environment is the key.

Interaction with a new object causes dendrite growth, but once the novelty wears off, growth subsides. In the cages intended for learning, toys are changed and rearranged daily. There are toys for stimulation of many senses: bells, running ladders, things with odors. "Every day," Greenough notes, "the rat faces a novel, challenging environment."

Diamond's group wanted to see if it were possible to carry this too far. In a four-week study, they tried changing the toys every hour for part of the night. There were no significant increases in dendrite growth in the brains of these rats over those whose toys were changed

Every time we do something to challenge our mind or body,
we are building brain power.

once a day. "The rats didn't have time to assimilate information that was coming in," Diamond says. So switching constantly from one activity to another, without giving our brain any down time, will probably not contribute to increased learning capacity.

Experience matters. It can change the very structure of the brain, the way its cells connect. And it can do so throughout our lifespan. The best thing we can do for our brain is to offer it challenges, social interaction, and active participation in both physical and mental activities.

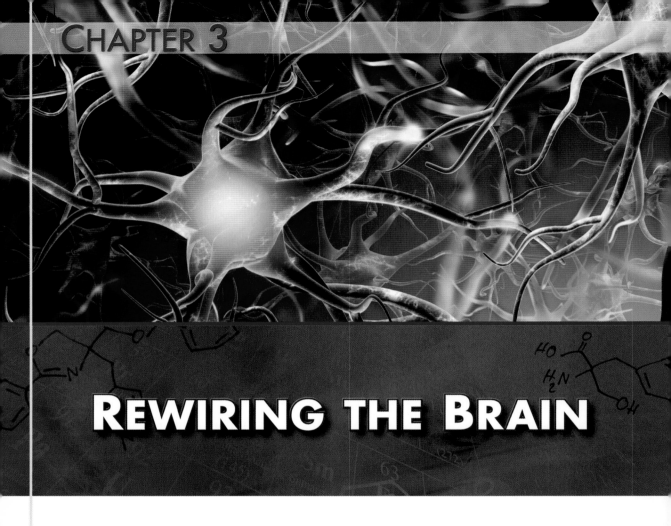

CHAPTER 3

REWIRING THE BRAIN

Can you teach an old brain new tricks? The answer lies in brain "plasticity"—the brain's adaptive response to change.

BRAIN WIRING 101

Packed inside your brain are one hundred to two hundred billion neurons with dendrites. Stimulating a neuron's dendrites sends an electrical signal through the cell body. This signal may cause an impulse that will be carried down a neuron's tail-like axon away from the cell body. The brain's neurons could light a 60-watt bulb, but that's not their job. Instead, the brain controls almost everything your body does.

As previously explained, to do that, neurons form connections, primarily by "synaptic" transmission. Chemical neurotransmitters released at axon ends cross synaptic clefts. The chemicals stimulate receptors on other neurons at synapses.

Each neuron can make up to ten thousand connections. Most two-year-olds' brains have twice as many neuron connections as adults'. Unused connections disappear as the brain matures.

Fifteen years ago, people thought that the brain became fully "wired" by age three. Now scientists know that the brain isn't mature—with all its specialized systems in place—until age twenty.

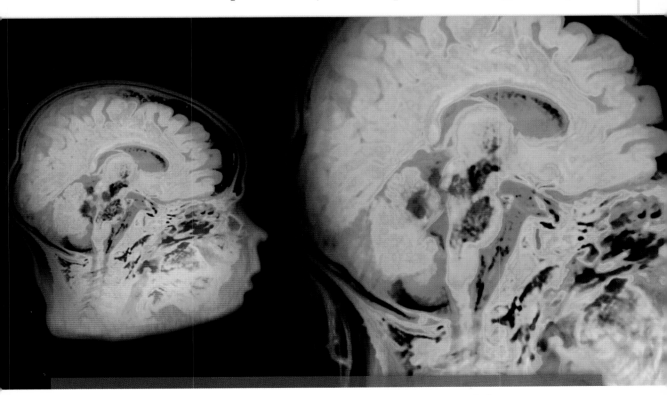

This MRI compares the brain of a child (*left*) and an adult (*right*) as they listen to someone speaking. The areas in blue are the part of the brain activated by hearing speech.

"If you look at the brain of an adult, it's a highly specialized mosaic of systems and subsystems," notes Helen Neville at the University of Oregon. "There are a lot of local connections, but also long distance connections." Some brain systems process sight and sound. Others interpret language, feel emotions, or control spatial representations.

NATURE VS. NURTURE

Genetic information controls a lot of brain development. Thus, most adults process visual information in the occipital lobes near the back of the head. Frontal lobes behind the forehead process conscious thoughts.

Although blind people can't process visual information, they still use their occipital lobes when they read braille. Braille is a system of writing using raised dots in specific patterns to represent letters, numbers, special characters, and whole words.

Yet genes can't explain everything. "There are hundreds of trillions of connections in the brain, and there isn't nearly enough information in the genes to specify that information," explains Neville. "There's a very important role for input from the environment in shaping brain systems."

Studies of people born deaf, for example, show that they process visual information not only with the occipital lobes, but elsewhere as well, including parts normally used for hearing. Basically, they adapt to deafness by expanding the brain system for sight. Similarly, people born blind use parts of their occipital lobes in reading braille.

Another study comparing London taxi drivers' brains to other people's showed growth in the hippocampus. The hippocampus plays an important role in spatial memory, which taxi drivers need to remember routes in a crowded city.

Brain changes also occur as people learn to play the piano, study languages, or acquire other skills. In other words, says Mriganka Sur at the Massachusetts Institute of Technology, "the brain is different after learning than it is before."

CRITICAL PERIODS

"Some brain systems retain the ability to change throughout life," notes Neville. "But other brain systems really require input at specific times or they never develop normally."

Learning to perceive depth properly requires appropriate input from both eyes during the first year. This means pediatricians should try to correct "wandering eye" very early for babies.

As this baby walks, his brain is learning depth perception, as well as fine-tuning gross motor skills and balance.

People can learn vocabulary words throughout life. However, elementary school children learn sounds and internalize grammar rules of a second language better than adults. The earlier students learn a second language, the better they'll do.

Scientists are examining what critical periods may govern math, music, and other skills. Their research will likely shape how children study in school.

SPEEDING RECOVERY

After accidents or strokes cause brain injury, other parts of the brain sometimes take over functions of damaged areas. "We're just beginning to understand how the body and the brain recover from injury and how we can manipulate those processes," says Michael Weinrich at the National Institute for Neurological Disorders and Stroke. Because of new discoveries about brain plasticity, "there are all sorts of very exciting applications on the horizon."

One study restricted stroke patients' unaffected sides so that they'd use their partially paralyzed hands more. Faster recovery rates suggest such therapy speeds growth of new neuron connections.

Can brains be rewired manually? Following specific guidelines to prevent any pain or suffering, Massachusetts Institute of Technology researchers "rewired" young ferrets' brains so that visual signals went to areas which normally interpret sound. Afterward, the ferrets' vision was normal.

"This argues for a tremendous amount of plasticity," notes Sur. Such surgery isn't likely in humans anytime soon. Nonetheless, the research suggests we can do much more to stimulate brain plasticity. Who knows what lies ahead?

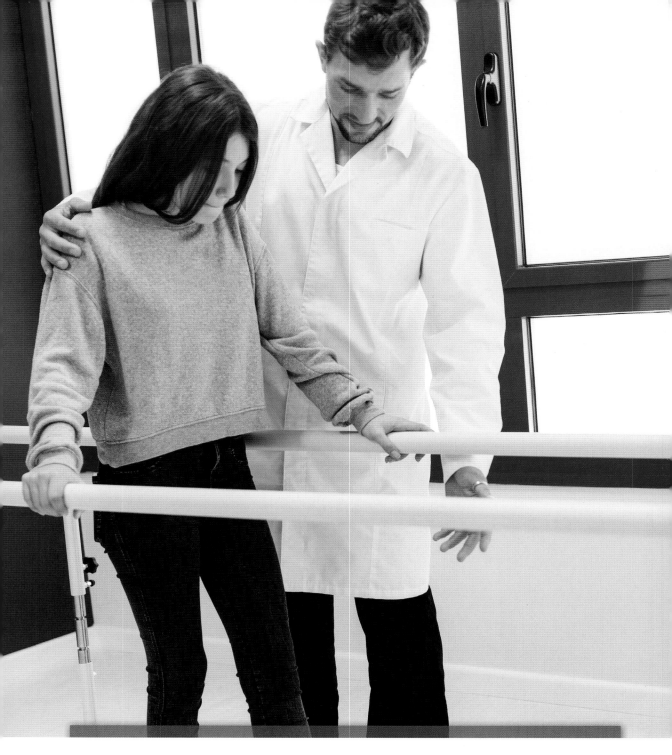

Physical therapy can help retrain the brain to move certain body parts after the brain has been damaged in some way.

Rather than dealing with injuries to the brain, it is better to take safety precautions to prevent them. Seat belts and helmets help prevent injuries to your head in case of accidents.

MAINTAIN YOUR BRAIN

Brain plasticity isn't unlimited, so take care of your developing brain. Wear seat belts in cars. Strap on helmets and other protective sports equipment.

Remember, too, that tobacco, alcohol, marijuana, and other drugs all interfere with neurotransmitters. Don't let these chemicals "rewire" your brain and hinder your intellectual, emotional, and social growth.

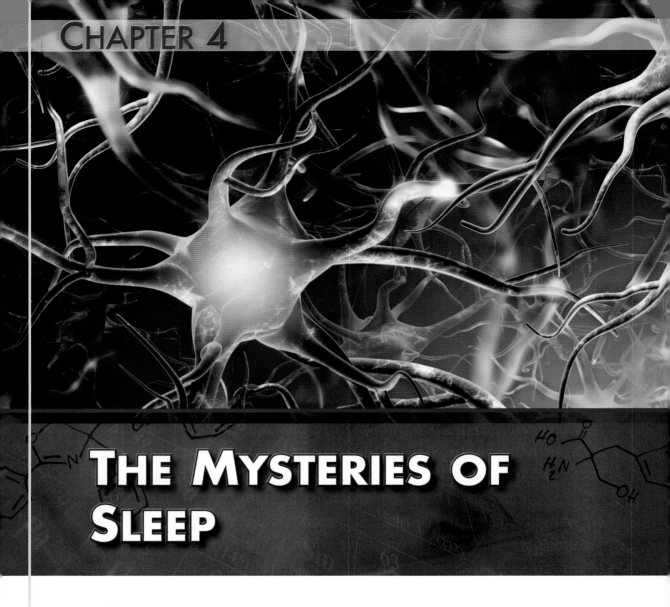

CHAPTER 4

THE MYSTERIES OF SLEEP

Guess what you'll spend one-third of your life doing. Sleeping! Believe it or not, if you live to be seventy-five, the hours you sleep each night will add up to about twenty-five years of slumber.

It might seem like all that sleep is a giant waste of time. But scientists now know that while you're snoozing quietly in your bed, there's lots going on inside your brain and body.

CYCLING THROUGH SLEEP

For one thing, you sleep a cycle of five different types of sleep, over and over each night. When you first lie down and begin to fall asleep, your body enters what sleep experts call Stage 1 sleep. You're still very close to being awake, but your brain begins to work more slowly. Your body relaxes, and your closed eyes start to roll around. If someone woke you from this stage, you'd probably say that you weren't even asleep yet. After several minutes, you sink a little deeper, into Stage 2 sleep. You'd still be easy to wake up, but you'd probably know you'd been snoozing.

During sleep, our bodies work to build up the immune, muscular, skeletal, and nervous systems.

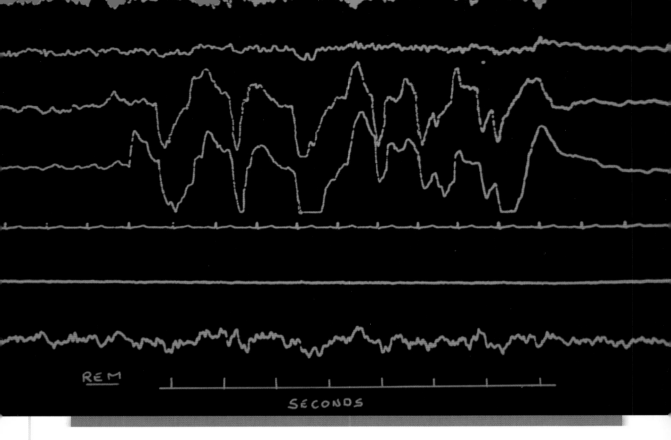

REM

SECONDS

This image shows the activity of the brain and different muscles, including the eyes and throat, during REM sleep.

Then you really relax and fall deeply asleep, into Stage 3 sleep. Your heart slows down, and you breathe more slowly, too. Noises nearby would probably not wake you. Finally, you sink into the deepest sleep of all, called Stage 4. Once you're in Stage 4 sleep, you're very hard to wake up. And if someone does manage to wake you, you'll be very confused about where you are and what's happening.

The first time you reach Stage 4 sleep after going to bed, you stay there for almost twenty minutes. That's the longest chunk of deep sleep you'll have all night. After that, you slowly move back up through Stages 3 and 2.

And then your sleep gets *really* interesting.

SWEET DREAMS

As you come back up through a period of Stage 2 sleep, you shift into Rapid Eye Movement, or REM, sleep. It's called REM sleep because when you're in it, your eyes—behind your closed eyelids—slide quickly back and forth, and back and forth, as though you were watching the ball in a tennis game. Your brain becomes much more active during this sleep stage, almost as active as when you're awake. Instead of resting, a brain in REM sleep is racing! And while your eyes are darting from side to side, a very detailed story is running through your head: you're dreaming.

During REM sleep, your brain may create nonsensical dreams featuring fantastical worlds and strange people from bits and pieces of your waking life.

It's during REM sleep that you dream your strangest dreams, the ones that sound so very mixed-up when you describe them the next morning. As you drift into a REM-sleep dream of singing toothbrushes or a dog that says he's your uncle, your body changes, too. Your breathing and heart rate sometimes speed up. Scientists say that your brain waves—measurements of the electrical activity in your brain—look almost the same during REM sleep as they do when you're awake. When you enter REM sleep, you go from being completely relaxed to being ready for action. And yet, you never move. That's because you can't. You're paralyzed!

When you're in REM sleep, your brain cuts off all the messages that might tell your body to move. You never pull up the covers or even roll over. Except for your shifting eyes, your breathing, and a twitch every now and then, you lie perfectly still as you dream. Scientists guess that may be to prevent you from acting out any wild scenes in your dream and hurting yourself.

DOES DREAMING MAKE YOU SMARTER?

You'll spend more than two hours each night in REM sleep, dreaming. Why do you dream? Scientists are still trying to figure that out.

One idea is that dreaming helps you organize your memories. It gives your brain a chance to sort through everything that happened during the day, storing what you need to remember and tossing out details that don't matter.

Experiments show that REM sleep definitely can help you learn better. In one test, volunteers were taught a new skill. That night, some of them were awakened whenever they entered REM sleep. The others were awakened the same number of times but only during non-REM sleep. The next day, the people who got their REM sleep tested better than the others at performing the new skill.

Researchers now think dreams may be like exercise for your brain, and dreaming may actually help your brain develop. Newborn babies spend almost half of their sleep time in REM sleep! But adults, whose brains aren't developing so much anymore, spend only about one-fifth of their sleep time dreaming.

THE TICKLE TEST

When you're awake, you are aware of everything you hear, see, smell, touch, and taste. As you fall asleep, though, the part of your brain that passes on those messages stops sending the ones it decides you don't need to know about. That's why you may not hear your brother get up in the night to use the bathroom. Unless something is important, your brain ignores it.

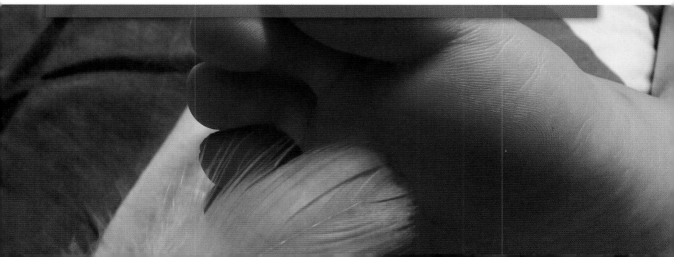

You can witness firsthand how the brain is selective about the events it deems important enough to wake you up for. Try tickling someone's feet while they're asleep and see if they wake up.

You can see how this works some evening when you're awake but your brother is sound asleep. Try tickling him with a feather or the edge of a soft cloth. Did he wake up? Or did he just brush the feather away while still sleeping?

Next, try talking to him. Say a few words in a soft voice. Probably he will continue to sleep. Now try saying his name once or twice. He's more likely to wake up at the sound of his name because it gets his brain's attention as an important sound.

YOU DREAM WHAT YOU SEE

Scientists aren't exactly sure why you have the dreams you do. But they do know that you dream about what you see when you're awake. In one experiment, volunteers who wore goggles with red lenses for twenty-four hours every day reported that, within a few days, all the objects in their dreams were red.

GOING WITHOUT SLEEP

During the day your muscles are busy stretching and pulling as you run, jump, or even just sit. Lying down asleep and fairly still gives those muscles a chance to repair and grow stronger. Scientists carried out an experiment on weight-lifters. For one night, they allowed the athletes to sleep only three hours. The next day, none of the athletes could lift as much weight as they had before. If you didn't sleep, you wouldn't be as strong either.

As you lie snoozing, you're busy healing and growing. Your body is releasing more of the chemicals that help it create new bits of skin, muscle, and other parts of you. Sleep is so important for healing

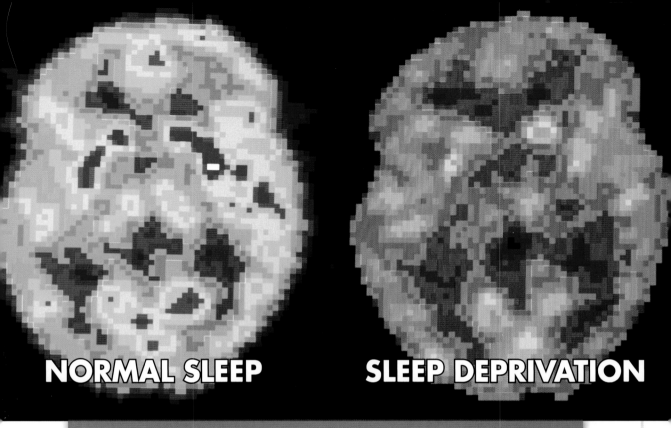

NORMAL SLEEP   **SLEEP DEPRIVATION**

The PET scan on the left shows a brain provided with normal sleep. The brain on the right was deprived of sleep. Red, orange, and yellow indicate areas of most activity, green means less activity, and purple shows areas of least activity. Sleep deprivation causes subdued brain activity, illustrated by the larger areas of purple.

that when you're injured or sick, your body releases chemicals to make you feel sleepier. Just recovering from a sunburn can make you sleep longer.

In one experiment, scientists kept a group of rats awake to study what would happen to them. After one week with no sleep, the rats began losing weight, even though they were eating more and more food. Their body temperatures dropped below normal, and cuts and scrapes wouldn't heal. After sixteen sleepless days, the rats died. Why?

Most animals, including you and those rats, have an immune system—a kind of defense force that fights disease-causing germs. Special cells in your immune system, such as T-cells, work every day to destroy germs that manage to slip inside you. When you sleep, your immune system has a chance to create more of those special germ-fighting cells. If you don't sleep as much, it can't make as many.

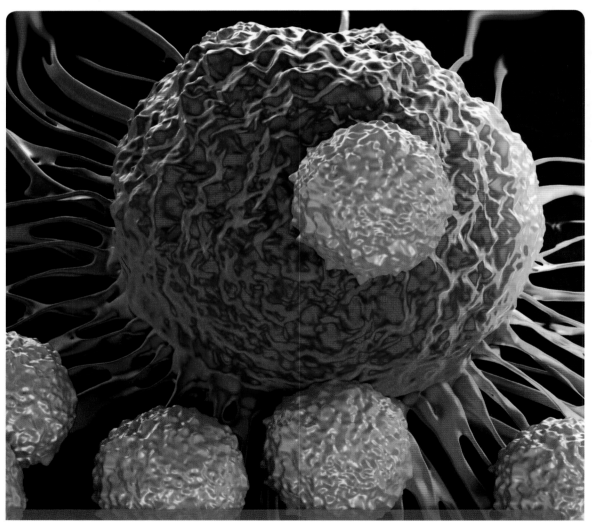

This illustration shows a T-cell attacking a cancer cell. Sleep is extremely important for maintaining the immune system, which fights disease.

When the scientists examined the sleep-deprived rats, they discovered that they had become infected by germs that their bodies could ordinarily fight off easily. But in the overtired rats, the infections had just grown worse and worse. Without sleep, the rats' immune systems couldn't do their job.

YOU'VE GOT RHYTHM

If you've ever been around newborn babies, you know that night and day don't mean much to them. They might be awake at three o'clock in the morning and asleep at four o'clock in the afternoon. It takes months for most babies to adjust to the rhythm of sleeping at night and being awake during the day.

But like most people, you probably feel wide awake in the morning, even if you went to bed late the night before. After lunch, you may begin to feel sleepy. In late afternoon, though, you perk up and feel wide awake again around supper. Then, just at bedtime, that sleepy feeling comes over you again. The regular pattern each day of wide-awake times and sleepy times is called your circadian rhythm.

Inside your brain, in the region where nerves carry the information from your eyes, are two tiny clusters of cells, each about the size of a pinhead. They're what scientists sometimes call your biological clock. These cells seem to keep track of the time. They let your body know when to produce chemicals to wake you up or make you sleepy. They keep your brain alert and ready to receive all the information your eyes, ears, and other parts of your body pass along. Then, as night comes, they work with different parts of your brain to stop making wake-up chemicals and start making sleep-time chemicals.

Almost every living thing follows its own special pattern of sleepiness and wakefulness in the twenty-four hours of each day. Bees do, for instance. They visit flowers to gather nectar only at a certain time of day. And many flowers open at the same hour every day, too.

SLEEP ON IT

Though there are still many mysteries to be solved about what goes on inside you during sleep, scientists know for sure that you need to sleep to keep your body healthy and your brain active. Missing

The bodies of sleep-deprived people will force them to take micronaps in the middle of working or studying in an effort to catch up with the sleep the brain needs to function properly.

just two hours of sleep one night will make you less alert the next day. You won't do as well in your schoolwork or physical activities.

And if you miss a whole night's sleep? Then you're really in trouble. You'll start to feel worried and unhappy. It might be hard to find the right words when you talk. You'll have difficulty concentrating and remembering, and your body might not be able to fight off germs.

Sleep is so important, your body makes sure it gets some. If you're tired enough, your body will make you fall asleep, even if you don't want to. Adults who don't get enough sleep often take tiny little naps of just a second or two called microsleeps. They don't mean to take these naps. Their bodies just take them the moment they're sitting still. In one experiment, researchers found that overtired people could fall asleep even when their eyes were held wide open with tape!

Scientists still can't explain why some people need more sleep than others, or why some animals get by with a lot less sleep than people can. But one thing's for sure: getting enough sleep will help scientists figure it out.

SET YOUR BIOLOGICAL CLOCK

Your body needs clues and reminders to help it stay on the right sleeping-waking schedule. When you eat your meals or brush your teeth at a regular time each day, that helps your body keep track of when it should make you sleepy or awake.

The most important clue for your biological clock, though, is light. When your body senses the light that shines in through your window in the morning, your brain was probably already preparing for you to wake up. The sunlight signals your brain that it's on the right track. Then, as the daylight begins to fade in the evening, your brain senses it and begins preparing for you to go to sleep.

When Thomas Edison invented the light bulb, people began staying up later. Before the light bulb, people slept about nine hours each night. Now most adults sleep only seven or eight hours. The effect of the artificial light on their biological clocks may be part of the reason.

As the light grows dimmer in the evenings, it sends a message to our brains to produce hormones that will help us go to sleep.

SLEEPING IN SPACE

When NASA sends the space shuttle on a mission, the astronauts inside it have some pretty complicated work to do. Sometimes that work has to happen at a time when the astronauts would normally be sleeping if they were still down on Earth. But they need to be wide awake!

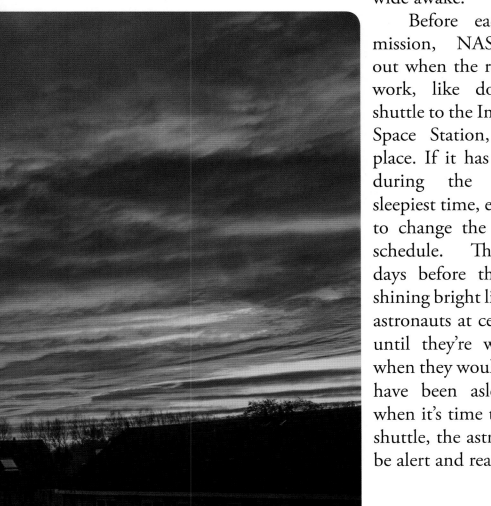

Before each shuttle mission, NASA figures out when the really tough work, like docking the shuttle to the International Space Station, will take place. If it has to happen during the astronauts' sleepiest time, experts have to change the astronauts' schedule. They begin days before the mission, shining bright lights on the astronauts at certain times until they're wide awake when they would normally have been asleep. Then, when it's time to dock the shuttle, the astronauts will be alert and ready.

Astronauts have to train their bodies to sleep at times that will be most convenient for the work they have to do on their missions. They also have to be strapped down so they don't float around and bump into things while they sleep!

These experts don't just shine light in an astronaut's eyes, either. A person's whole body senses light. In fact, experiments show that extra hours of light could throw off people's waking up and sleeping times even when that light was shone only on the skin at the backs of their knees!

BRAINS ARE BUSY!

As you can see, our brains are very busy. They are the control centers of our bodies and they are constantly changing and adapting based on what is happening to our bodies. They are even working to keep us healthy and help us learn while we are asleep! It seems important that we should take good care of our bodies and our brains, through trying new things, eating good food, drinking water, and getting plenty of rest—it is doing the same thing for us!

GLOSSARY

assimilate To absorb information and understand.

axon A long, wire-like part of a nerve cell that carries signals away from the cell body to other cells.

braille A writing system of raised dots read by the blind using their fingertips.

dendrite A short, branching structure of nerve cells that receive messages from other cells.

enriched Improved in quality or richness.

frontal lobe The part of the brain behind the forehead that controls reasoning, planning, parts of speech, movement, emotions, and problem solving.

hippocampus The part of the brain thought to control emotion, memory, and the autonomic nervous system.

impoverished Removed of quality or richness.

neuron A nerve cell that carries messages between the brain and other parts of the body and are the basic units of the nervous system.

neurotransmitter A chemical that transmits signals between nerve cells.

occipital lobe The part of the brain that controls vision and things related to vision.

plasticity The adaptability of an organism to changes in its environment.

synapse The tiny gap between two nerve cells through which signals jump from one cell to the next.

BOOKS

Deak, JoAnn, and Terrence Deak. *The Owner's Manual for Driving Your Adolescent Brain*. San Francisco, CA: Little Pickle Press, 2013.

Gifford, Clive. *The Human Brain in 30 Seconds*. Minneapolis, MN: Ivy Kids – Quarto Library, 2016.

Gold, Martha V. *Learning About the Nervous System*. Berkeley Heights, NJ: Enslow Publishers, 2013.

Holleben, Jan von, Michael Madeja, and Katja Naie. *That's What You Think! A Mind-Boggling Guide to the Brain*. Berlin, Germany: Little Gestalten, 2015.

Mooney, Carla. *The Brain: Journey Through the Universe Inside Your Head*. White River Junction, VT: Nomad Press, 2015.

WEBSITES

InnerBody: Nervous System
www.innerbody.com/image/nervov.html
Click on an interactive diagram to learn more about each part of the nervous system.

KidsHealth: Your Brain and Nervous System
kidshealth.org/en/kids/brain.html
Read facts and do activities related to the human brain.

Neuroscience for Kids
faculty.washington.edu/chudler/introb.html#bb
Explore the field of neuroscience through facts, games, and questions and answers.

INDEX